Computer and Social Media Misuse

By Daniel Barnett

The Employment Law Library

All books in the Employment Law Library are sent for free to members of the HR Inner Circle.

1. Employee Investigations
2. GDPR for HR Professionals
3. Preventing and Defending Employee Stress Claims
4. Employment Tribunal Time Limits
5. Deconstructing TUPE
6. Changing Terms & Conditions
7. Constructive Dismissal
8. Resolving Grievances
9. HR Hazards
10. Employment Status
11. Spotting Malingering
12. Employment Tribunal Compensation
13. Hiring Staff
14. Computer and social media misuse

Published by Employment Law Services Limited, Unit 3, Chequers Farm, Chequers Lane, Watford, Hertfordshire WD25 0LG

ISBN 978-1-913925-08-6

Acknowledgments

This is the fourteenth book in my series of mini guides on employment law for HR professionals.

As always, there are a number of people to thank. First and foremost, I'd like to thank David Appleton for his help with the content. I'd also like to thank Tincuta Collett for the layout and design, Aaron Gaff for proofreading and Maria Rodriguez for converting the book into the formats needed for Amazon.

Finally, I'd like to thank the members of the HR Inner Circle for whom I primarily write these small books (and who get them all for free as part of their membership). If you're interested in learning more about HR Inner Circle membership (www.hrinnercircle.co.uk), there is more information at the back of this book.

Daniel Barnett
January 2023

ABOUT THE AUTHOR

Daniel Barnett is a leading employment law barrister practising from Outer Temple Chambers. With 25 years' experience defending public and private sector employers against employment claims, he has represented a Royal Family, several international airlines, FTSE-100 companies and various NHS Trusts and local authorities. Employee clients include David & Victoria Beckham's nanny and Paul Mason (subject of the ITV documentary 'Britain's Fattest Man').

Daniel is a past chair of the Employment Lawyers' Association's publishing committee and electronic services working party. He is the author or co-author of eight books, including the Law Society Handbook on Employment Law (currently in its 8th edition). He is the creator of the Employment Law (UK) mailing list, an email alerter bulletin service sending details of breaking news in employment law three times a week to 33,000 recipients.

Legal directories describe him as 'extremely knowledgeable and [he] can absorb pages of instructions at lightning speed', 'involved in a number of highly contentious matters', 'singled out for his work for large blue-chip companies', 'combination of in-depth legal knowledge, pragmatism, quick response times and approachability', 'inexhaustible', 'tenacious', 'knowledgeable', and 'an excellent advocate'.

He is one of the leading speakers and trainers on the employment law and HR circuit. He has presented seminars for the House of Commons, the BBC, Oxford University, HSBC, Barclays Bank, Ocado, and dozens of other organisations in-house. In 2013, 2014, 2016, and 2019 he designed — and was the sole speaker at — the Employment Law MasterClass national tour.

As well as full-time practice as a barrister and speaker, Daniel is the founder of the HR Inner Circle – a membership club for smart, ambitious HR Professionals. In 2007, he co-founded CPD Webinars Ltd, then the UK's leading webinar training company for lawyers, and sold it to Thomson Reuters in 2011.

Daniel is widely sought after as a commentator in both broadcast and print media on all legal issues. Since 2010 he has presented the Legal Hour on LBC Radio. In 2019, he launched Employment Law Matters, a weekly podcast with short explanations of employment law topics. Subscribe at www.danielbarnett.co.uk/podcast

www.danielbarnett.co.uk
Temple, London

DANIEL BARNETT
BARRISTER

THE UK'S LEADING
YOUTUBE CHANNEL FOR
LAW EXPLAINER VIDEOS

WWW.YOUTUBELEGAL.CO.UK

Contents

All employment and HR practitioners are competing for work in a market where clients are more conscious of spend, and competitors from ABSs & large independent consultancies encroach into the market.

In Intelligent Marketing for Employment Lawyers you will discover how the internet can revolutionise the way you do business and generate new clients, as well as increasing fees and obtaining more work from existing clients.

Visit
GO.DANIELBARNETT.COM/BOOKS
for more information.

Chapter 1
Introduction

There can be very few employers nowadays which do not utilise information technology (IT) in some way or other. Computers started to regularly appear in UK workplaces in the mid-eighties, and they have now become as ubiquitous as pens and paper; maybe even more so!

However, IT is merely a tool, and like many tools, it can be dangerous if used incorrectly. Add to that the huge growth of social media both in and outside of the workplace, and there is the potential for the perfect storm.

This publication examines how IT and social media can be misused in the workplace by both employees and employers, the damage it can do and the practical and legal safeguards that can be put in place to mitigate the risks.

Chapter 2 offers an overview of some of the key issues that can arise from the misuse of IT and social media. The chapter is divided into two main parts – **misuse by employees**, and **misuse by employers**. The subsequent chapters then look at the main issues in more depth, from both a legal and a practical point of view.

Please note that in this publication, the terms 'employee' and 'employer' are used as a convenient way to describe the relationship between all the types of individuals who work in or for an undertaking, whether they are legally employees or not. Many of the issues addressed can equally involve employees, workers, contractors, agency staff or volunteers, and most of the guidance therefore relates equally to them all, but where the legal status of a person matters, this is made clear. For a detailed examination of the differences between the various categories of personnel, consult Book 10 in the Employment Law Library: 'Employment Status', published in May 2021.

Chapter 2

An overview of misuse

Employee misuse

The following are examples of the types of conduct by an employee that can cause headaches for an employer. Some of them overlap and can be of varying degrees of seriousness.

- misuse of the employer's IT system and/or social media accounts to bully or harass colleagues, managers or others

- unauthorised or excessive personal use of the employer's IT system

- using the IT system to steal or misuse the employer's confidential information or intellectual property

- endangering the employer's IT system by deliberately or negligently introducing malware

- misuse of the employer's IT system or social media accounts to damage its reputation

- employees using their own IT equipment and/or social media accounts in their own time to bully or harass co-workers, managers and others associated with the workplace

Some of these types of conduct can amount to a criminal offence, whilst others may give rise to civil liability for both the employee and the employer. These issues are explored in detail in Chapters 3 to 9.

Employer misuse

Assuming that an employer does not deliberately set out to bully, harass or defame an employee or damage them in some other way, the main areas of risk arising from an employer's use of IT are in the realms of discrimination, data protection and privacy, so that their use of IT could lead to:

- breaches of data protection legislation in relation to their employees, which can arise from how personal information is gathered and used, and the extent of that information

- invasions of employees' privacy, which can arise from the monitoring of employee's communications and activities using 'bossware' or other methodologies

- over-reliance on, or misuse of, artificial intelligence resulting in discrimination and unfair dismissal risk, which can arise from the use of algorithms to make decisions about employees

These issues are examined in more detail in Chapter 10.

Chapter 3
Cyberbullying and harassment

Obviously, **bullying and harassment** can take many forms, but the misuse of technology to bully and harass has become particularly prevalent for a combination of reasons, including:

- the ubiquity of technology in almost every aspect of our working and personal lives, giving abusers a plethora of opportunities

- the temptation to hide behind a screen, which takes less courage than face-to-face bullying

- the sharp increase in remote working, where people's actions are subject to less immediate scrutiny

- the mental health impacts of the Covid-19 pandemic, pushing people to behave badly

Whatever the reasons, the impact of cyberbullying is no less serious than more traditional types of bullying and harassment and, in some cases, it has a greater impact. Whereas the victim of conventional bullying and harassment can usually escape from it when they leave work (although not necessarily mentally), victims of cyberbullying and harassment can experience it at any time of the day or night, including in the sanctity of their own homes.

Let's first consider what bullying and harassment are.

Bullying

There is no statutory or definitive definition of bullying, but the **Advisory, Conciliation and Arbitration Service (ACAS) defines bullying in the workplace** as unwanted behaviour from a person or group that is:

- offensive, intimidating, malicious or insulting, or

- abuse or misuse of power that undermines, humiliates or causes physical or emotional harm to someone

ACAS says that bullying may:

- be a regular pattern of behaviour or a one-off incident

- happen face to face, on social media, in emails or on calls

- happen at work or in other work-related situations

- not always be obvious or noticed by others

ACAS gives the following examples of bullying at work:

- spreading a malicious rumour about someone

- regularly putting someone down in a public setting

- regularly giving someone a heavier workload than everyone else

- putting humiliating, offensive or threatening comments or photos on social media

- undermining a manager by showing continued disrespect, refusing to complete tasks, spreading rumours or making the manager seem unskilled or unable to do their job – ACAS refers to this as 'upward' or subordinate bullying

Many of these examples can occur both in person and through the medium of technology and social media. For example, cyberbullying can include:

- a manager or supervisor criticising or undermining a staff member publicly by copying in colleagues to a critical email or message. Whilst this form of bullying may lack the immediate impact of the victim being directly humiliated in front of colleagues, it is arguably equally as damaging, or worse, because the criticism is in writing, and so is permanent, and it can easily be disseminated to others, including outside of the organisation. In addition, it can be sent at any time of the day or night, so the victim cannot escape.

- failing to copy someone into an email or message sent to all other members of a team, thereby undermining them, or ostracising them. Again, this can be quite a public gesture, as the absence of the victim's name from the recipient list may be obvious.

- sending insulting or inappropriate messages or images directly to someone.

- sending insulting or inappropriate messages or images about someone to others or posting them on message boards and social media platforms. This is often done via social media platforms such as Facebook. It may be the employer's own Facebook page or a private page.

Harassment

Harassment is formally defined in **section 26 of the Equality Act 2010**. It can be summarised as follows (conflating subsections (1) and (2)):

> *"A person (A) harasses another (B) if A engages in unwanted conduct related to a relevant protected characteristic, or of unwanted conduct of a sexual nature, and the conduct has the purpose or effect of violating B's dignity, or creating an intimidating, hostile, degrading, humiliating or offensive environment for B."*

There is a further definition in subsection (3) relating to less favourable treatment where B rejects or submits to unwanted conduct of a sexual nature or that is related to gender reassignment or sex, and A treats B less favourably than A would treat B if B had not rejected or submitted to the conduct.

In other words, **harassment is a form of bullying that amounts to unlawful discrimination**, and bullying legally becomes harassment when it is related to one of the protected characteristics defined in the Equality Act 2010. These are the inherent characteristics of a person that may be the cause of them suffering unlawful discrimination.

The protected characteristics as listed in the Equality Act 2010 are:

- sex
- marital or civil partnership status
- race
- gender reassignment
- religion or belief
- sexual orientation
- pregnancy or maternity leave
- age
- disability

It is helpful to understand these protected characteristics in a little more detail, and they are defined in the Equality Act 2010.

Sex specifically refers to a male or a female of any age. Sex for these purposes does not include gender reassignment or sexual orientation. The Equality Act 2010 was drafted before the current greater awareness of fluid gender identity, so it does not, on its face, protect someone who identifies as a gender other than that assigned at birth.

Marital or civil partnership status refers to someone whose marriage is legally recognised in the UK and someone whose civil partnership is registered under the Civil Partnership Act 2004. The status of being unmarried or single is not protected, even if the person was once married or in a civil partnership. An intention to marry or enter into a civil partnership also does not confer any protection.

Race is defined as including colour, nationality and ethnic or national origins. A racial group will share colour, nationality and/or ethnic or national origins (such as British people, Black British people, or South Asians) and can also be made up of more than one racial group. Nationality refers to the legal relationship between a person and a state through birth or naturalisation, whilst national origins must have identifiable elements, both historic and geographic. For example, the Scottish have a separate national origin to the English.

Ethnic origin refers to an ethnic group defined by the courts. The ethnic group must regard itself and be regarded by others as a distinct and separate community because of certain characteristics, including a long-shared history and a cultural tradition of its own. A common language, literature, religion and/or geographical origin, amongst other things, can also be present. Sikhs, Jews, Roma, Irish Travellers, Scottish Gypsies and Scottish Travellers have all been confirmed by the courts to be ethnic groups capable of protection.

Gender reassignment refers to people who are proposing to undergo, are undergoing or have undergone a process (or part of a process) to reassign their sex by changing physiological or other attributes of sex. It is not necessary for someone to undergo a medical process to be protected, and someone who starts the process but stops partway through is also protected. Someone who 'cross-dresses' for reasons of gender identity is also protected.

Religion or belief includes any religion and religious or philosophical belief, as well as a lack of such religion or belief. To count as a protected religion, the religion must have a clear structure and belief system. Sects or denominations within a religion may count as a religion under the Equality Act 2010.

A belief must affect how a person lives their life, and must:

- be genuinely held

- not merely be an opinion based on the state of information available

- be a weighty and substantial aspect of human life and behaviour

- attain a certain level of cogency, seriousness, cohesion and importance

- be worthy of respect in a democratic society, not be incompatible with human dignity and not conflict with the fundamental rights of others

Humanism, atheism and ethical veganism have been found to count as protectable philosophical beliefs.

Sexual orientation refers to a person's sexual orientation towards persons of the same sex, the opposite sex or either sex. People can be protected in relation to their appearance, the places they visit and the people they associate with.

Regarding **pregnancy or maternity leave**, the Equality Act 2010 protects a woman from being treated unfavourably because of her pregnancy or related illness, or because she is exercising, has exercised or has sought to exercise her right to maternity leave. The protection lasts from the date when the woman becomes pregnant until she returns to work or the end of her maternity leave period, whichever is earlier. Outside of that protected period, unfavourable treatment because of her pregnancy would be discrimination because of sex.

Age is defined by reference to a person's age group, which can mean people of the same age or range of ages. Such groups can be wide (such as 'young people') or narrow (such as 'people born in 2000'), and the meaning can differ depending on the context.

Disability is defined in the Equality Act 2010 by reference to a disabled person:

> *A person (P) has a disability if—*
>
> * *P has a physical or mental impairment, and*
> * *the impairment has a substantial and long-term adverse effect on P's ability to carry out normal day-to-day activities.*

'Long-term' in this definition means that the impairment has lasted, or is likely to last for at least 12 months, or for the rest of the person's life. People who used to have a disability under this definition continue to be protected after the disability has ceased. Cancer, HIV infection and multiple sclerosis are deemed disabilities from the point of diagnosis, as they are progressive conditions that get worse over time in certain circumstances.

Examples of harassment

Any one of the examples of bullying given above can become harassment if it is carried out because of a person's protected characteristic.

Examples of harassment using IT could include:

- sending messages to or about someone that are offensive in a way that relates to a protected characteristic

- making avatars of colleagues that refer to a protected characteristic

- posting offensive comments about someone on social media in a way that relates to a protected characteristic

There are an unlimited number of ways IT can be used, and detailed rules about this may best be stated in the employer's bullying and harassment policy rather than the IT user policy.

Consequences of cyberbullying and harassment

Before looking at the legal risks and consequences, it is worth remembering that bullying and harassment in any form can have other **significant tangible and intangible costs**. These can include:

- adversely affecting the morale, and consequently the productivity, of the victim and of others who witness the bullying

- stifling diversity, innovation and creativity because people are afraid to 'be different'

- triggering retaliatory behaviour

- undermining management

- threatening health and safety

- damaging the reputation of the employer through whistleblowing allegations and anonymous negative reviews on sites such as Glassdoor

- increasing sickness absence

- increasing staff turnover

In addition, of course, there are **legal consequences of bullying and harassment** that can have serious reputational and financial impacts, as well as burdening managers with having to defend claims. The following sections explore some of those legal risks.

Constructive dismissal

If there is no connection between the unwanted behaviour and the victim's protected characteristics (so that the behaviour cannot be shown to be harassment), then the victim has a limited recourse in law, as there is no free-standing claim of 'bullying' or 'disadvantage' available in the UK. However, an employee (but not a worker) may be able to resign and claim constructive dismissal.

Constructive dismissal occurs where the employer has committed a **breach of contract** that is serious enough to 'repudiate' the contract; that is, to give the employee the choice of either ending the contract (in legal terms, 'accepting' the breach) or ignoring the breach and continuing in employment (often called 'affirming' the breach). To end the contract, the employee would have to resign, usually without giving notice. To succeed, the employee has to resign without undue delay (to avoid affirming the breach). The employee can then claim any losses arising from the breach of contract – normally the notice pay they would have received had they not had to resign without notice. They can also treat any future express obligations, such as post-termination restrictive covenants, as no longer applying to them (although confidentiality obligations remain). An employer bullying or harassing an employee would normally be serious enough to amount to a repudiation of the contract because a fundamental term – the duty of trust and confidence – would have been breached.

To succeed in a claim of **constructive unfair dismissal**, the employee must have been continuously employed for at least two years, ending with the effective date of termination, unless the repudiatory conduct by the employer was for a reason that grants an employee the right to claim automatic unfair dismissal, such as bullying because of someone's trade union activities. Constructive unfair dismissal is expressly recognised in section 136(1) of the Employment Rights Act 1996, which makes clear that the employee has to have been entitled to terminate the employment without notice (which does not preclude a resignation on notice) by reason of the employer's conduct.

Where **cyberbullying is carried out by the employer itself**, through the actions of a manager acting within the scope of their responsibilities, say, the victim could succeed in a claim of constructive dismissal if they could show that the bullying was so bad that it fundamentally breached the duty of trust and confidence owed by the employer to the employee. Merely using the IT system to performance manage an employee, say, may not cross the high threshold needed to succeed in a claim.

However, **where the cyberbullying has been carried out by a co-worker without the consent of the employer**, the victim would have to show that the employer knew about the bullying and did not do enough to protect them. In other words, it would not be the bullying itself that gave rise to the repudiatory breach, but the employer's failure to stop it or prevent it. The failure would have to be so bad as to breach the employment contract in a fundamental way. The following section examines the steps an employer can take to preempt this kind of risk.

Harassment and discrimination claims

Both an employee (using the legal definition of the term) and a worker (but not independent contractors or volunteers) can bring claims of **direct and indirect discrimination, victimisation and harassment in the workplace**. Direct discrimination and harassment are the most likely claims arising out of bullying-type behaviours. Indirect discrimination is explored in Chapter 10, which covers the use of artificial intelligence by employers.

Liability can lie with both the employer and an individual employee, such as the harasser or a manager that facilitates or ignores the harassment. Even if the employer does not instruct an employee to act in a discriminatory way, or does not endorse or condone the conduct, the employer can still be liable for the discriminatory acts, unless it can show it took '**all reasonable steps**' to prevent the action. If the employer can establish that defence, the employee may still be personally liable.

To be able to establish this defence, an employer should provide:

- an induction for new staff (including workers, agency staff and contractors) into the employer's bullying and harassment, IT usage, social media and disciplinary policies

- a more thorough induction for supervisors and managers into the contents of the policies upon their hiring or promotion

- regular reminders to all staff about the contents of the policies through internal newsletters and other means of communication

- periodic refresher training for all staff

- a clear reporting protocol for staff who wish to raise concerns

- a robust protocol for quickly investigating and addressing concerns about bullying and harassment

If an employer can show that they have carried out most or all of these steps, they would be in a strong position to defend claims of harassment and discrimination, as well as constructive unfair dismissal claims.

How to respond to a complaint about cyberbullying or harassment

For a thorough explanation of **how to conduct an investigation and disciplinary hearing**, see Book 1 in the Employment Law Library series: 'Employee Investigations'. In brief, though, it is recommended to take the following steps (not necessarily in this exact order):

- take a thorough statement from the complainant as soon as possible.

- work out what acts of misconduct may have been committed before accusing the alleged bully/harasser. Do this by reference to your relevant policies.

- appoint someone who is not closely connected to either the complainant or the alleged bully/harasser to lead the investigation. The person leading the investigation should have experience in conducting investigations and have the time to give the investigation their proper and prompt attention.

- decide who would be the decision maker if disciplinary action becomes necessary and who would hear any appeal.

- outline the process to be followed to the complainant and the alleged bully/harasser.

- ensure the alleged bully/harasser is aware of exactly what they are accused of, the process to be followed and the possible outcomes. A comprehensive letter setting these details out is essential.

- decide whether to suspend the alleged bully/harasser, ensuring you have a proper basis for doing so.

- establish whether there are any witnesses and if so, take statements from them.

- take possession as soon as possible of the laptop or device of the alleged bully/harasser. If it belongs to the individual, then suspend their access to your system and preserve all communications between the alleged bully/harasser and the complainant.

- take copies of and preserve all other relevant evidence.

- work out whether a criminal offence may have been committed and, if so, decide whether to contact the police by discussing the matter with the complainant.

- give the alleged bully/harasser the right to be accompanied to any meeting by a colleague or trade union representative.

- pass the results of the investigation to another person who will be the decision maker.

- the decision maker should make their decision on a balance of probabilities, having considered all relevant evidence and the employer's policies and procedures.

- give a right of appeal if any disciplinary action is decided upon.

- communicate the decision to the complainant, while respecting the privacy of the alleged bully/harasser.

- keep copies of all materials from each stage of the process in case a legal claim ensues.

This process is indicative only, and it should be kept under review. It is a dynamic process and flexibility is important. An overly rigid approach can lead to unfairness for both the complainant and the alleged bully/harasser.

Chapter 4
Unauthorised personal use of an employer's equipment and IT system

This topic tends to give rise to two main concerns:

- the employee wasting time carrying out personal activities during working hours, such as surfing, conducting personal business, engaging in social media and so forth. This is a concern that has come into sharp focus since remote working has soared in popularity. The risks of employee monitoring are addressed in Chapter 10.

- the employee misusing the employer's IT system to actively harm it, such as by competing with it. This is explored in Chapter 5.

Wasting the employer's time can take many forms, of course, and using the employer's technology is just one way of doing so. The issues divide into two:

- how much time an employee spends on their own tasks during work time

- what they actually do using the system

It is for the employer to decide how much it will tolerate **personal use** of its IT, and the employer needs to make any limits clear in its IT usage policy. In roles where employees are responsible for doing their work in their own ways, without rigid adherence to time scales and targets, employers may decide to give their staff a certain amount of leeway, provided the work is given priority.

There is no right or wrong approach, of course, but one mistake to beware of is having rigid rules in a policy which are not honoured in practice, as this will undermine any attempt later to enforce the rigid rule. It could lead to unfair dismissal and discrimination claims if an employee can show that others have been allowed to do things that the employee has been disciplined for. We recommend, therefore, that policies are regularly reviewed and reflect actual up-to-date acceptable practice. If an employer decides to change its practice, it should make clear what the change is going to be and when it will take place, and it should give reasonable notice of the change.

What the employer will allow an employee to do (as opposed to how much personal use it will allow) can impinge upon the security and integrity of the employer's system. Downloading apps and programs that could infect the employer's system must, obviously, be forbidden, and it is better to impose a blanket ban, unless the download is authorised, than to leave it to the employee to decide what is risky and what is not. In addition, some employers do not allow staff to access certain websites (such as gambling sites) for policy reasons and, again, the employer needs to make the rules very clear in its policies, although the employer can put in place blocks preventing access to such sites.

Chapter 5
Misuse of confidential information

Cases predating the 2000s tended to focus on employees making photocopies of their employer's confidential information, such as client lists and commercially sensitive data, and infringing their intellectual property, such as breaching their copyright and registered trademarks and passing off. The same underlying issues arise nowadays, except that such information tends to be emailed to personal email accounts or downloaded to memory sticks. The intent is the same; only the methods have changed.

Putting in place technological methods to protect confidential information is the best approach, as prevention is always better than cure. In addition, an employer limiting access to its confidential information to those who need to use it, rather than the information being readily available for anyone to see it, will bolster the employer's arguments in any injunctive action against a rogue employee that the information was confidential and worthy of protection.

Legal action in response to an employee misusing IT to steal confidential information includes seeking an injunction to prevent further misuse, called a **prohibitory injunction**, although it is also possible to get an injunction forcing an employee to do something, such as returning or deleting information. This is called a **mandatory injunction**.

Either type of injunction can be granted on an interim basis, and this is a very common application to make. It is a temporary measure to protect the employer's position until a full trial of the matters can be held. An interim injunction is usually sought at the same time as the claim is issued and served, although it can also be applied for prior to a claim where there is an urgent need to protect the employer's position.

Whether or not the interim injunction is granted, the matter will need to go to full trial at a later date, where all the evidence will be heard, and a **permanent injunction** may be granted.

In order to succeed in getting an injunction, the employer has to show that:

- there is a serious issue to be tried. This is not a high threshold, and the employer does not need to show it is more likely than not to win at trial.

- damages alone would not be adequate to protect the employer. Where the employee has kept confidential information and is using it against the interests of the employer, but the employer cannot yet calculate what damage that will cause, damages will not be adequate. On the other hand, if, for example, all the information has been deleted and there is no prospect of further misuse, then the injunction will not be granted.

- the 'balance of convenience' favours the employer. This means the court decides whether the employee would be more prejudiced by the granting of the injunction than the employer would be prejudiced by the injunction not being granted.

Before an interim injunction is granted, the court will need to be satisfied that the employer has given an undertaking as to damages. This is because the court does not examine all the evidence at the interim stage. If, at the end of the full hearing, it turns out that the interim injunction was granted wrongly, and the employee suffered loss and/or damage as a result, then the employer's undertaking will be relied on to compensate the employee.

Applying to the court for an injunction is a time-consuming business, and it can cost several tens of thousands of pounds in legal fees. If the employer ultimately loses, then it would also have to pay the employee's legal costs (or a reasonable proportion of them) as well, possibly, as damages pursuant to its undertaking. It is therefore very important to thoroughly assess the merits of your case and the risks of losing before applying for an injunction. There may be other ways of resolving the issues, such as:

- agreeing with the employee that they will return and/or delete the information in return for the employer not taking legal action

- deciding that the employee using the information will not harm the employer in any material way

- mitigating potential losses by contacting clients, suppliers and so on to ask them to stay loyal to the business

Of course, sometimes an employer needs to send a signal that dishonest action by employees will not be ignored, in which case taking legal action may be the most suitable approach, despite the cost.

Chapter 6

Endangering an employer's IT system

Deliberately damaging an employer's hardware, software or systems would likely constitute a criminal offence as well as serious misconduct justifying summary dismissal. The criminal aspects of computer misuse are examined in Chapter 9. Most problems arise, though, from careless or innocent mistakes by employees, without any intent to cause damage. However, this can still give rise to disciplinary action if the employer's expectations have been made clear and have been ignored.

Protecting your systems

Of key importance is the regular raising of awareness for all staff about the risks of cyberattacks. These can take many forms and are no longer necessarily simple to spot. Long gone are the days when we all had a laugh at the badly spelt emails from an overseas 'prince' offering access to millions of dollars in return for a 'fee'. Nowadays, there is an array of potential attacks that exploit various weaknesses in an organisation's

IT system, including the use of malware, ransomware, hacking and phishing scams.

Phishing is of particular importance as it can be a Trojan horse to enable wrongdoers to infiltrate systems without sophisticated hacking. Phishing often utilises the gullibility of staff and involves the sending of a fake or deceptive message attempting to fool the recipient into revealing sensitive information. 'Spear phishing' involves a targeted communication that purports to be from an important client, colleague or senior manager (where the sender's email address fakes that of a known and trusted person). Such communications are often sent out of hours so that the recipient cannot easily check legitimacy with the purported sender, and often ask for sensitive information or funds to be sent urgently. Spear phishing is relatively easy to carry out, and it is made even easier when an organisation publishes recipients' contact details and job roles on public websites. 'Whaling' is the targeting of senior executives and high-profile individuals through phishing.

These methodologies rely on the natural tendency for staff to want to be helpful or to do as they are told. Regular reminders for staff to be on the lookout for anything unusual are the best approach to raise awareness.

Should staff who fall for phishing attacks be disciplined? It is wise to be cautious. If there has been a clear breach of a policy, then it may be appropriate. However, often, phishing attacks work because the communications have been convincing. An otherwise careful and responsible employee who has been fooled by an ostensibly genuine request may instead be asked, in a non-blaming way, to assist their employer to understand how they were duped to prevent future occurrences.

Apart from the use of policies (see Chapter 8) and training to set boundaries and raise awareness, an employer should also have a range of other measures in place to mitigate the risks, which can encompass the wider issues arising from cybersecurity threats. Whilst a detailed examination of these measures is beyond the scope of this publication, in brief, these could be as follows:

- implementing technical processes to help prevent misuse, such as firewalls and other malware prevention software, the use of virtual private networks, offline and cloud backup systems and physical security measures. The National Cyber Security Centre (NCSC) has a range of tools available on its website to help organisations defend themselves against attacks.

- keeping up to date on the latest threats. The 'Mitre ATT&CK' knowledge base identifies the latest tactics, techniques and procedures used by attackers to compromise data.

- carrying out regular audits and risk assessments.

- developing an action plan about how to respond appropriately to an attack, including an HR and/or legal response, a data recovery protocol and/or a reputation damage limitation exercise.

- insuring against loss and damage caused by employee misuse. This could be part of a wider insurance policy that addresses cybercrime in general.

Data protection issues arising from a cyberattack

An employer who has been the subject of a cyberattack has **duties under the data protection legislation** to determine whether the incident has led to a personal data breach. This could be the unlawful or accidental destruction, loss, alteration or disclosure of personal data. In a ransomware attack, the unlawful encryption of personal data can cause timely access to the data, which is also a data protection breach in law.

If a data protection breach has occurred, the employer must **notify the Information Commissioners Office** (ICO) without undue delay, and within 72 hours, unless the breach is unlikely to result in a risk of adversely affecting the rights and freedoms of individuals. Where the breach is likely to result in a high risk of adversely affecting individuals' rights and freedoms, you must also inform the individuals without undue delay.

Detecting breaches requires robust breach detection, investigation and reporting procedures. Where there is a breach, in order to assess whether you need to notify the ICO and individuals, you must undertake a formal risk assessment, and keep a record of the data breaches and the risk assessment, even if notification is not necessary.

The ICO website has a personal data breach assessment tool to help you identify reportable personal data breaches.

As well as notifying the ICO, you may determine that it is worth advising law enforcement agencies.

Chapter 7
Misuse of computers and social media outside of work

It is clear that an employee who breaches the employer's IT and social media policies at work may be disciplined and, if appropriate, fairly dismissed. As ever, clear rules must be set out in the employer's social media and disciplinary policies. However, what is the position when the employee has used their own computer and social media accounts to commit an act that the employer considers to be unacceptable?

It has been established for many years that an employee can be disciplined, and even dismissed, for misconduct that occurs outside of the workplace, provided that the misconduct has some material impact on the employment relationship. This may occur if the employee has made their position untenable because clients or colleagues refuse to work with them, for example, where an employee has been convicted of downloading child pornography at home. Another example could be where the employee has posted material online that maligns the employer or members of management or staff.

Examples of cases involving Facebook

Dismissals have been found to be fair in a range of situations involving employees making public and private posts on Facebook that insult either the employer company or members of management. The case law can be a little hard to reconcile though. In one case, an employer was found to have been fairly dismissed when he repeatedly referred on Facebook to his workplace as "Dante's Inferno", and then refused to take the post down, using a swearword (*Weeks v Everything Everywhere Ltd*, ET/2503016/12). Whereas, an employee who posted on Facebook that "This place of work is beyond a fucking joke", and that he would soon be "doing some busting" was found to have been unfairly dismissed (*Trasler v B&Q* ET/1200504/12).

Comments made on Facebook to a closed circle of the poster's friends can lead to a fair dismissal provided that the employer does not breach the employee's Article 8 rights to privacy and Article 10 rights to freedom of expression or, if it does, the breach is justified and proportionate in order to protect the employee's reputation. See *Crisp v Apple Retail (UK) Ltd* ET/1500258/11.

Merely liking a comment made by someone else has been found not to justify dismissal where there was no evidence of lasting reputational damage. See *Blue v Food Standards Agency* ETS/4100341/14, where the employee had liked a comment about his manager being attacked.

Where an employee expresses views that their employer does not agree with, dismissal is likely to be unfair unless there is an impact on the employee's ability to do their job. See *Smith v Trafford Housing Trust* [2012] EWHC 3221, a case involving an employee who expressed disapproval of gay church marriages in a Facebook post.

Chapter 8
Use of policies and other measures to protect the employer

Employees learn an awful lot in their first few months on the job, including about the culture and expectations of the workplace. This is important, and often cannot be replaced by instructing them to read dozens of pages of a handbook or manual. However, even the most laid back and 'regulation-lite' employers will need to set boundaries and behavioural expectations, and this is where well-drafted and relevant policies come in.

Whilst a lot of the rules and expectations in a workplace will either be obvious and intuitive or quickly learned, many will have developed over time or will depend on the personal views of managers and owners. These rules and expectations will often vary widely across work groups, businesses and industries and an employer cannot therefore reasonably expect an employee to know or intuit exactly what is acceptable and what is not. This is particularly the case in respect of usage of the employer's IT system and social media.

A good HR policy addressing IT and social media usage will set out what is expected and what is not allowed, giving examples. It will describe the penalties for failure to abide by the policy and will cross-refer to other policies, such as those dealing with confidentiality, data protection and bullying and harassment, to ensure consistency across all policies. The amount of detail in the policy will depend on the amount of trust the employer places in their employees and how complex the systems and rules are. The two overlapping areas of IT usage and social media usage can either be contained in the same policy, or two separate policies may be adopted.

On the whole, a detailed policy is preferable because it leaves less to interpretation and inference, but employers may want to avoid being overly prescriptive or restrictive, as such an approach tends to damage staff morale and cause resentment. An approach that is built on trust and explains the risks of non-compliance is more likely to work.

What might a typical IT usage policy contain?

An IT usage policy may contain the following sections:

- a description of the classes of people it applies to. The policy should apply to anyone who has access to the IT system, including agency staff and contractors. Naturally, different categories of staff may have access to different parts of the system, but this should be made clear, so that any unauthorised personnel attempting to access sensitive areas can be disciplined or terminated, as appropriate.

- rules about the use of the employer's IT systems, including the extent of any permitted personal use; unauthorised access and use; and the use, downloading and uploading of software.

- rules about access to and use of the internet using the employer's equipment and IT systems.

- rules about the use of the employer's equipment and maintaining its security, including the use and sharing of passwords. These rules may include care of the equipment, restrictions on what equipment may be removed from the premises, the use of flash memory devices, the downloading and uploading of data and programs to devices, the locking and/ or shutting down of devices when not in use, and the prompt reporting of damage or loss.

- rules about the use of an employee's own devices at work, including the downloading of the employer's confidential information and deletion of the employer's data and programs upon leaving.

- rules about using the employer's communications systems, such as emails, messaging services and mobile phones, including the extent of any permitted personal use, monitoring of employees' usage and expectations of privacy, attaching files, and caution to be exercised when receiving communications from third parties.

- rules about remote access and remote working. These may focus on ergonomic and health, safety and welfare issues, the securing of the employer's equipment and the protection of confidential information.

- rules about the expected etiquette when communicating internally and externally using the employer's systems. This may include the content of emails and messages and the use of video conferencing systems.

- cross-references to other policies, such as harassment and bullying, confidentiality, and data protection.

- a brief explanation of the relevant law in relation to potential criminal acts arising from an employee's misuse of the employer's IT and communications systems.

- a description of the disciplinary options open to the employer for breach of the policy.

- a description of who is responsible for the policy and contact details for any questions arising.

- a date for review of the contents of the policy, usually around two years hence.

The **social media policy** may contain the following sections:

- a description of the classes of people it applies to. As above, the policy should apply to anyone who has access to the employer's social media platforms, but as the policy may extend to the activities of staff on their own private social media insofar as it affects the employer, it needs to make clear that all classes of people are included.

- a list of the employer's social media accounts to which the policy applies.

- a prohibition on employees using the employer's social media accounts unless authorised. Usually, only authorised people will have access to the accounts in any event.

- rules about the topics that authorised employees may post about and guidelines on acceptable and unacceptable content. This guidance may be quite detailed, as a firm's official Facebook, Twitter and LinkedIn accounts, and so forth, are its shop windows, and the messages may need to be very carefully crafted.

- where relevant, such as for firms subject to the Financial Conduct Authority's regulations, the policy may need to expressly prohibit certain activities that are subject to regulatory restrictions, for example, where the disclosure of inside information may manipulate the market by affecting the prices of shares in a public listed company, and other financial instruments.

- rules about monitoring employees' usage of the employer's social media accounts. This is to give the employer the right to oversee employees' activities.

- rules about unacceptable references to the employer, managers, directors, shareholders, customers and other staff in employees' personal social media accounts. It is important to cross-reference this section of the policy to other policies covering bullying and harassment and the disciplinary policy.

- if relevant, a statement that the employer monitors public posts on the personal social media accounts of staff to ensure compliance with the rules of the policy. On its face, there is nothing to stop an employer monitoring the public posts of staff. However, an express statement that it does so may help to avoid allegations of intrusive prying into employees' private lives.

- a brief explanation of the relevant law in relation to potential criminal acts arising from employees' misuse of the employer's social media accounts.

- a description of the disciplinary options open to the employer for breach of the policy.

- cross-references to other relevant policies.

- a description of who is responsible for the policy.

- a date for review of the contents of the policy, usually around two years hence.

Policies are not just pieces of paper

A policy is useless if it is simply written down and then filed away. It should be treated as a **living document** that helps employees and managers understand their employer's expectations and conduct themselves accordingly. This means that a policy has to be understood, first and foremost, by those that have to implement and enforce it. Managers and supervisors should be in a position to explain any part of the policy that falls within the ambit of their responsibility.

As with all policies, new employees should therefore be carefully taken through the IT and Social Media policies, effectively being trained in their content, and then asked to sign to confirm they have read and understood their content. Each policy should be reviewed, and updated as necessary, on a regular basis.

Many employers now use self-guided programmes to train staff on the contents of important policies, and then to test their understanding of the policies. Apart from saving time, this approach creates an objective record of what the employee actually understands about the contents of the policies.

Chapter 9
Criminal offences

Few employees, or employers for that matter, consider the criminal side of misconduct involving the misuse of social media or an employer's IT system. This chapter reviews the main pieces of legislation that are directly relevant to the misuse of an employer's IT system.
In addition, there are criminal offences that can be committed using an employer's IT system and/or social media platforms.

Computer Misuse Act 1990

Unfortunately, it is not unknown for employees to use their employer's IT system in unauthorised ways to carry out various acts of misconduct. For example, a disgruntled employee may seek to get revenge on their employer, a manager or a colleague for a perceived slight or wrongdoing. Or, an employee may want to use the system to their own advantage. There are three main offences under the Computer Misuse Act 1990 that are worth examining:

- using a computer to access a program or data in an employer's IT system. Employees may do this for all sorts of reasons, including reading, stealing or disseminating confidential information; sending malicious communications; sabotaging a colleague's work; or amending timesheets and other personnel records.

- impairing the operation of a computer or program, or preventing or hindering access to a program or data. Examples include deleting, corrupting or encrypting programs, files or data, or introducing some other form of malware that causes the system to crash or become unavailable.

- accessing the system to commit other offences, such as financial crimes or harassment.

Each one of these actions could amount to a criminal offence, and summary conviction can attract up to 12 months' imprisonment or a fine. Conviction on indictment can attract terms of imprisonment of between two and 10 years, depending on the offence committed.

It is also an offence to make, adapt or supply any article enabling someone to commit an offence under the Computer Misuse Act 1990. So, supplying someone with malware to enable them to sabotage their employer's system would fall under this offence. Conviction on indictment for this offence can carry a maximum term of imprisonment of two years.

For a person to be found guilty, the court would have to be satisfied that the action in question was unauthorised (which may not always be easy to prove in an employment situation) and, as with most criminal acts, that there was an intention to do the act at the time it was done (called 'mens rea'). The court would have to be satisfied beyond all reasonable doubt that the offence was committed.

Cases are rarely prosecuted under the Computer Misuse Act 1990, but one such case was in 2018 when a motor industry employee was sentenced to six months' imprisonment for having accessed thousands of customer records containing personal data without permission, using colleagues' login details. The employee used the information to make nuisance calls to the customers. The Information Commissioner's Office brought the prosecution.

Even though prosecutions are rare, we recommend that IT user policies refer expressly to the Computer Misuse Act 1990, and criminal offences referred to in this chapter, to deter staff.

What if an employer accesses an employee's personal laptop, remotely for example, in order to check their work and accidentally finds personal information? It is unlikely that this would be found to be a breach of the Computer Misuse Act 1990 provided that the employer had a published policy allowing it to access devices used by an employee for work purposes.

The Malicious Communications Act 1988

The Malicious Communications Act 1998 addresses the situation where one person sends another person a communication conveying a message that is indecent or grossly offensive, a threat or information that the sender knows or believes is false. Where these actions are done with the purpose of causing distress or anxiety to the recipient, an offence is committed for which a term of imprisonment on conviction on indictment of up to two years and/or a fine may be imposed.

The making of a threat that is used to enforce a demand made on reasonable grounds where the sender reasonably believes that the use of the threat was a proper means of reinforcing the demand does not constitute an offence.

In the context of the workplace, an offence could be committed by an employee emailing or messaging another person, whether within the workplace or outside of it (including speaking by telephone or leaving a voice message). Managers could also fall foul of the Malicious Communications Act 1998 if using written or electronic communications to bully an employee. It does not matter how the message is sent, whether via email, a text-based messaging system, a hard-copy letter, a voice message, a telephone call or social media, to name but a few.

It is worth noting that there is no requirement for the communication to be received by the intended recipient, as it is the act of sending the communication (with the accompanying intention of causing distress or anxiety) that constitutes the offence.

As with the Computer Misuse Act 1990, prosecutions are few because of the public interest concerns of suppressing free speech. It is suggested that only really egregious cases are likely to end up before the courts. Again, though, it is recommended that employers bring this piece of legislation to the attention of employees as a deterrent.

There are also legislative provisions that criminalise certain behaviours using **social media**. Trolling, online threats, disclosure of private sexual images without consent, online harassment, grooming, online stalking and virtual mobbing may all constitute criminal offences. Two key offences involve the Communications Act 2003 and the Prevention from Harassment Act 1997.

Section 127 of the Communications Act 2003

Section 127 prohibits the use of public electronic communications equipment to send a message that is false, grossly offensive or of an indecent, obscene or menacing character. This is punishable by up to six months imprisonment or an unlimited fine or both. The section also prohibits the sending of a communication through a public network intended to cause annoyance, inconvenience or needless anxiety to the recipient.

The sender must intend the prohibited effect, but there is no requirement for the message to be received, or for anyone to see the communication or be offended by it.

A workplace example is an employee who uses Facebook, Instagram, Twitter, YouTube or the like to send an objectionable message or threat to a colleague or manager.

As with the other offences, the threshold for criminal liability is high, with the threats or offensive comments being assessed objectively. Two non-work-related examples of successful prosecutions are of note. One involved a man attaching messages to YouTube videos threatening violence to two identified individuals, and death to categories of people. The other involved a woman posting hyperlinks via a blog of herself singing grossly offensive anti-Semitic songs. Even though the links were not directed at anyone in particular, they were deemed to be communications within the meaning of the section.

The Prevention from Harassment Act 1997

The Prevention from Harassment Act 1997 covers harassment in general, but it can include harassment that is carried out using electronic means. The

Prevention from Harassment Act 1997 prohibits someone from "pursuing a course of conduct which amounts to harassment of another, which he knows or ought to know amounts to harassment". It is also prohibited to harass two or more individuals with the intention of persuading a person to do or not do something.

References to harassing a person include alarming a person or causing the person distress. In the case of harassment of one person, a "course of conduct" must involve conduct on at least two occasions. In the case of harassment of two or more persons, the conduct must occur on at least one occasion in relation to each person.

Putting someone in fear of violence is also an offence under the Prevention from Harassment Act 1997.

The Prevention from Harassment Act 1997 also prohibits stalking amounting to harassment, which includes electronic stalking, and is defined as follows:

- following a person
- contacting, or attempting to contact, a person by any means
- publishing any statement or other material—
  - relating or purporting to relate to a person, or
  - purporting to originate from a person

- monitoring the use by a person of the internet, email or any other form of electronic communication

- loitering in any place (whether public or private)

- interfering with any property in the possession of a person

- watching or spying on a person

The police may obtain a warrant to enter premises and seize material that could be admissible as evidence to prosecuting an offence of stalking. This could extend to IT equipment being seized from an employer's premises.

Clearly, these definitions can encompass situations where an employee uses their own or their employer's IT system or a public social media platform to harass co-workers, managers and others associated with the workplace.

Imprisonment and fines may be imposed for breaches of the Protection from Harassment Act 1997, and injunctions and awards of damages for distress caused may be issued. A person may be acquitted of an offence but still be made the subject of an order of the court to protect someone from harassment by that person.

Hate crimes

Someone who demonstrates or is motivated by hostility towards someone based on race, religion, disability, sexual orientation or transgender identity can be guilty of a **hate crime**, under the **Crime and Disorder Act 1998**. Section 66 of the **Sentencing Act 2020** allows prosecutors to apply for an uplift in sentence for someone convicted of a hate crime. The Crown Prosecution Service website states that they use an everyday understanding of the word hostility, which includes ill-will, spite, contempt, prejudice, unfriendliness, antagonism, resentment and dislike.

Chapter 10
Employer misuse of IT systems and social media

There are three main areas of activity where an employer can get itself into hot water:

- activity that breaches data protection legislation

- activity that invades the privacy of employees

- misuse of or overreliance on artificial intelligence algorithms

Data protection

The activities of most employers will result in them harvesting a vast amount of personal information about their employees, almost all of which will be held on the employers' IT systems. This process of data gathering and retention starts at the recruitment phase and continues throughout the lifetime of an employer's association with an employee. It may even extend beyond the employee's leaving, when requests for references are received, and the personal data is likely to be held for several months, if not years.

The types of personal data collected and held by an employer will typically include:

- CVs, completed application forms, equal opportunities monitoring responses, proficiency and psychometric test results, emails, texts and messages with candidates, social media searches, interview notes, offers of employment, references and draft employment contracts

- pay data, next of kin information, health data

- training records, performance reviews, sickness and leave records

- disciplinary records, including investigations, letters and other communications

- termination data

- reference requests and responses

The employer will be a **data controller** for the purposes of the legislation and, as some of the information will be sensitive (known as 'special category data'), it is crucial to understand the consequences of receiving and holding all that data.

Problems may arise when an employer collects or uses:

- personal data without the knowledge of the employee

- personal data for a reason that has not been fully explained to the employee

- more personal data than they legitimately need

- personal data that is inaccurate

- personal data for longer than is necessary

- personal data in a way that endangers its security

For example, if the employer receives information about an employee's private life from a third party, which they keep on file without telling the employee and which is not relevant to the employee's job within the organisation, that is likely to show a breach of data protection legislation by the employer.

Another risk results from the employer having inadequate security measures to stop personal data being accessed by people with no authority. A typical breach that occurs frequently is an employer keeping information longer than they need to.

There are two pieces of legislation in the UK that currently deal with data protection. The retained EU law version of the **General Data Protection Regulation** (known as the UK GDPR since 1 January 2021) and the Data Protection Act 2018. Please note that the government is currently reviewing the UK's data protection laws, with a view to making them more business-friendly, although at the time of writing, they had not yet published the results of the public consultation process that closed in November 2021.

It is important to begin by defining some key terms.

Personal data is any information relating to an identified or identifiable living individual. This encompasses a potentially vast range of information in an employment context, such as names, contact details, schools attended, qualifications, work history, affiliations, health conditions and other personal characteristics, to name but a few.

A data subject is an identifiable living person to whom personal data relates. Anyone about whom the employer holds personal data will be a data subject and subject to the protections of the UK's data protection laws. This includes employees, agency staff, workers, volunteers and independent contractors amongst others.

A data controller is a natural or legal person, public authority, agency or other body that alone or jointly determines the purposes and means of processing personal data. This will include all employers.

Processing means carrying out an operation or set of operations on personal data, either manually or automatically. This definition has a very wide scope and includes (by way of example only):

- collecting, recording, organising and storing data

- retrieving and using data

- adapting, amending or combining data

- transmitting, disseminating or otherwise disclosing or making data available

- restricting, destroying or amending data

Special category personal data relates to sensitive information, of which processing is prohibited unless an exception applies. Such data includes information about:

- racial or ethnic origin

- political opinions

- religious or philosophical beliefs

- trade union membership

- genetic data

- biometric data for the purpose of unique identification

- health data

- data about a person's sex life or sexual orientation

Whilst most employers would not deliberately choose to collect and otherwise process some of these types of special category data, it is possible to end up with them accidentally.

Special circumstances apply in relation to processing personal data relating to criminal convictions and offences.

Because of the very wide definition of processing and of personal data, an organisation employing and engaging staff will fall within the scope of the legislation. This means that the organisation will have to comply with the seven **data protection principles**. These principles can be summarised as follows:

- personal data must be processed **lawfully, fairly and in a transparent way**.

- personal data must only be collected for **specified, explicit and legitimate purposes** and must not be processed any further in a way that is incompatible with those purposes.

- personal data must be **adequate, relevant and limited to what is necessary** in relation to the purposes for which it is processed.

- personal data must be **accurate** and, where necessary, **kept up to date**. Inaccurate data must be **rectified or erased**.

- personal data must be **kept for no longer than is necessary** for the purposes for which it is processed.

- personal data must be processed in a way that **ensures appropriate security**, including protection against unauthorised or unlawful processing, accidental loss, destruction or damage.

- the principle of **accountability** requires that the data controller is responsible for and must be able to show compliance with the other principles.

In what situations can an organisation process personal data? The UK GDPR allows processing in six situations only. These are called the **Article 6 conditions**. The four that are likely to be relevant to recruitment are where:

- the data subject has **given consent** to the processing of their personal data for one or more specific purposes.

- the processing is **necessary for the performance of a contract** to which the data subject is party or in order to take steps at the request of a data subject prior to entering into a contract.

- the processing is **necessary to comply with a legal obligation** to which the controller is subject.

- the processing is **necessary for the purposes of the controller's legitimate interests** or those pursued by a third party, except where those interests are overridden by the interests and fundamental rights and freedoms of the data subject which require protection of personal data.

Consent is not considered a safe condition to rely on in an employment scenario because employment relationships are not based on an equality of power, meaning the consent to process personal data may not be seen as a freely given, specific, informed and unambiguous indication of the data subject's wishes.

It is not safe to argue that consent is implied when a job candidate or employee discloses personal data, as they will not necessarily know exactly how it will be stored, who will see it and how it will be used. It is always better to try to rely on one of the other reasons.

The performance of a contract condition is one relied on significantly by employers in relation to their existing staff, and the pre-contractual limb of it may be relevant in a recruitment scenario when an offer has been made and negotiations are ongoing between the preferred candidate and the potential employer.

Compliance with legal obligation will include statutory, regulatory and common law obligations that the employer is subject to. This could include pre-employment vetting to ensure that the candidate has the right to work in the UK or ensuring that an employee has a valid driving licence.

The legitimate interests category is arguably the most flexible for employers. Because of the limitations inherent in this category, in relation to the interests and fundamental rights and freedoms of the data subject, processing carried out for this reason must be done proportionately and in the least intrusive way possible.

The ICO guidance identifies that, in order to use this reason, the controller must:

- identify a legitimate interest, which could be its own or another person's, including the data subject's

- show that the processing in question is necessary to achieve that legitimate interest

- balance its legitimate interest against the individual's interests and fundamental rights and freedoms

An example could include collecting information about an employee's qualifications and experience. The processing could typically include storing the information, extracting parts of it, copying the information to managers or supervisors, and then later deleting it. The legitimate purpose for processing this information could be to enable the employer to assess the candidate's suitability for promotion or training. The processing as described is necessary to achieve that legitimate interest and is not likely to infringe on the employee's fundamental rights and freedoms.

However, let's say an over-enthusiastic manager copies the employee's CV to his entire department of 40 people, asking for feedback and comments about the employee's bid for promotion. That is likely to fall outside the scope of what one could regard as necessary to achieve the legitimate interest of assessing suitability. The action would likely be seen as excessive and disproportionate, and as something that should not occur.

Where an employer holds **special category personal data** about an individual, the employer must ensure that the appropriate conditions are met (set out in Part 1 of Schedule 1 of the Data Protection Act 2018. The conditions are:

- the processing is **necessary for the purposes of performing or exercising obligations or rights** which are imposed or conferred by law on the employer or employee in connection with employment.

- when the processing is carried out, **the employer has an appropriate policy** in place.

- the employer must **keep a record of processing activities**, including the following information:

  ○ that the condition relied on is that processing is necessary for the purposes of performing or exercising obligations or rights of the employer or data subject that are imposed or conferred by law

- whether the personal data is retained and erased in accordance with the employer's policies, and if not, the reason

- how one or more of the Article 6 conditions are met

These safeguards, along with those relating to the policy document, are known as the **Part 4 additional safeguards**.

The **policy document** referred to must explain the employer's procedures for complying with the data protection principles in connection with the processing of the data and must explain the employer's policies regarding the retention and erasing of personal data, indicating how long the data is likely to be kept.

For the period beginning when the employer starts to carry out processing and ending six months after the employer ceases such processing, the employer must:

- retain the appropriate policy document

- review the policy document and update it as appropriate

- make the policy document available to the ICO, without charge, upon request

These requirements are also part of the **Part 4 additional safeguards**.

An example of an employer legitimately processing special category personal data in a recruitment context is where a role has certain health requirements, such as a certain level of eyesight or hearing ability.

Another condition enabling the processing of special category personal information relates to **race equality**.

An employer may also process special category personal data (including data about an individual's criminal convictions and offences committed) where the employee or candidate has **given their express consent**, or where one of the **substantial public interest conditions** set out in Part 2 of Schedule 1 of the Data Protection Act 2018 has been met (provided that an appropriate policy document is in place, along with the additional safeguards set out in Part 4 of Schedule 1 of the Data Protection Act 2018).

The **substantial public interest conditions** are:

- administration of justice

- preventing fraud

- terrorism or money laundering

- equality of opportunity or treatment

- specific circumstances

Most of the substantial public interest conditions are unlikely to apply in most workplace situations.

However, the condition relating to **equality of opportunity or treatment** could apply where the data reveals racial or ethnic origins, religious or philosophical beliefs, health concerns or sexual orientation. The processing must be for the purpose of identifying or reviewing the existence or absence of equality of opportunity or treatment between specified groups, with a view to enabling such equality to be promoted or maintained. In addition, this exception does not apply where:

- the processing is carried out for the purposes of measures or decisions regarding a specific data subject

- the processing is likely to cause substantial distress or damage to an individual

- the data subject has served written notice to stop processing their personal data

Another specific public interest condition is set out in paragraph 9 of Part 2 of Schedule 1 of the Data Protection Act 2018, where the processing is carried out as part of a process of identifying suitable individuals to hold senior positions in an organisation. A senior position is a director, secretary or similar officer, a member of an LLP, a partner or a senior manager who has a significant role in making decisions about how an organisation's activities are to be managed or organised.

Privacy notices

In their capacity as data controllers, recruiters and employers have an obligation under the UK GDPR to provide information to candidates and staff (whether employees, contractors or agency workers) about any personal data about the candidates or staff that the employers are collecting and processing. There is no prescribed way of doing this, but the most convenient way is probably to issue a privacy notice (also known as a fair processing notice).

The privacy notice has to include the following information:

- the organisation's name and contact details

- the names and contact details of the organisation's representative and data protection officer

- the purposes of processing the personal data

- the lawful basis for processing the personal data

- what legitimate interests you are relying on

- the categories of personal data

- where the personal data will be obtained from

- who will receive the personal data

- details of any transfers of the personal data overseas

- how long the personal data will be kept

- the rights of the individual in relation to the processing of the personal data

- the right of the individual to withdraw consent to the processing of their personal data, if consent has been given

- the right of the individual to complain to the ICO

- details of whether the individual is under a statutory or contractual obligation to provide the personal data (if it is collected from the individual it relates to)

- details of any automated decision making, including profiling, if relevant

This information must be given to the individual when you collect personal data from them, or within a month of obtaining it if you get it from another source. If you plan to disclose the personal data to a third party, the individual must be advised of that no later than when the information is disclosed.

There are some exceptions to when you have to provide privacy information, including where the individual already has it, where it would be impossible to provide it, or where it would involve a disproportionate effort. You can also withhold the information if doing so would render the achievement of the objectives of the processing impossible or seriously impair it. This would be where you are recording the movements of staff in order to try to detect who is responsible for a spate of thefts, for example.

The privacy information you provide must be concise, transparent, intelligible, easily accessible and use clear and plain language. In other words, you must not use technical jargon or be misleading, and you must ensure that the information is easy to locate.

Because the privacy notice has to be "meaningful", it must be tailored for the type of business, the kind of personal data being processed, how the personal data is processed and the individuals it will be given to. For example, the notice you would give to employees is likely to be quite different from the notice you would give to casual independent contractors, for whom far fewer types of information are likely to be held.

Bossware

When lockdowns spread throughout the world, Zoom became a household name and remote working became the new normal, reports started to emerge about what has become known as 'bossware' – tracking and analytics software used by employers to monitor the productivity of staff. There are a number of bossware packages on the market, in several countries, that enable employers to track, amongst other things:

- what an employee is doing, such as applications used, websites visited, subject lines in emails sent and so forth.

- how productive an employee is, such as how many keystrokes or clicks per minute they make using keylogging software

- the location of an employee using GPS data on smartphones and in company vehicles

- whether an employee is physically sitting at their device

- what an employee is saying

There is no doubt that some of this software produces useful data for both the employer and the employee and that the data can be used constructively by both to help the employee use their time more effectively. It may even be used to encourage a better work/life balance.

Clearly, tracking software like this needs to be used judiciously and not relied upon to discipline or disadvantage employees without a more thorough investigation being undertaken. For example, bossware may be very sophisticated in its operation, but it can give a very misleading picture of an employee's productivity. If an employer concludes that an employee who has not typed anything during working hours for 30 minutes has been shirking, they may have ignored the fact that the employee was on the phone with a client or colleague discussing work, or even using pen and paper to create a mind map, say.

In addition, there is a real danger that employer surveillance can impinge significantly on the privacy of the employee. Some software can be used to activate the camera and microphone of devices, which, whilst designed to check the employee is working, can inadvertently capture images and conversations of a private nature. For example, the employee's children may be photographed or filmed without the employee's permission or knowledge, or conversations with their intimate partner captured.

Where the employee is authorised to use the employer's system for private purposes, such as sending personal emails or accessing websites for personal reasons, the software will not be able to differentiate between work and private usage, and so will capture authorised private usage indiscriminately.

All of these outcomes create risk from a data protection point of view, which was examined in the data protection section, above. Part 3 of the ICO's Employment Practices Code expressly addresses the monitoring of employees at work. The Code recognises that the data protection legislation does not prevent monitoring, and that monitoring may be necessary in some cases to satisfy the Code's requirements. However, any adverse impact of monitoring on individuals must be justified by the benefits to the employer and others.

The ICO's Employment Practices Code sets out the following core principles in relation to workplace monitoring:

- it will usually be intrusive to monitor your workers.

- workers have legitimate expectations that they can keep their personal lives private and that they are also entitled to a degree of privacy in the work environment.

- if employers wish to monitor their workers, they should be clear about the purpose and satisfied that the particular monitoring arrangement is justified by real benefits that will be delivered.

- workers should be aware of the nature, extent and reasons for any monitoring, unless (exceptionally) covert monitoring is justified.

- in any event, workers' awareness will influence their expectations.

The ICO's Employment Practices Code describes how to judge whether any adverse impact of monitoring on individuals is justified by the benefits to the employer and others by carrying out an 'impact assessment'.

An impact assessment involves:

- identifying clearly the purpose(s) behind the monitoring arrangement and the benefits it is likely to deliver

- identifying any likely adverse impact of the monitoring arrangement

- considering alternatives to monitoring or different ways in which monitoring might be carried out

- taking into account the obligations that arise from monitoring

- judging whether monitoring is a proportionate means of achieving a legitimate aim

Offences arising out of surveillance and monitoring

The **Investigatory Powers Act 2016** makes it a criminal offence to intercept a communication during the course of its transmission by means of a public or private telecommunication system, where the interception is carried out in the UK and the person intercepting does not have lawful authority to carry out the interception. This prohibition extends to computer and telephone networks in the workplace if they are attached to a public system. Therefore, if an employer monitors transmissions made by a telecommunication system, the employer must have lawful authority to do so.

A communication can be lawfully intercepted under the Investigatory Powers Act 2016 if the person doing the intercepting has reasonable grounds for believing that both the sender and the recipient have consented to the interception. This would work if the employer had obtained the consent, through the employment contract for example, for it to intercept emails sent between employees. It may be harder to satisfy the condition where the sender or the recipient is outside of the employer's organisation. Interestingly, because of the way the concept of interception is defined in the Investigatory Powers Act 2016, it is likely that an employer opening emails that have already been opened by the intended recipient would not constitute an interception.

However, the **Monitoring and Record-Keeping Regulations 2018** allow interception without consent in a business context in order to:

- establish the existence of facts

- ascertain compliance with the regulatory or self-regulatory practices or procedures relevant to the business

- ascertain or demonstrate standards that are or ought to be achieved by persons using the system

- prevent or detect crime

- investigate or detect the unauthorised use of the telecommunications system

- ensure the effective operation of the telecommunications system

The Monitoring and Record-Keeping Regulations 2018 also allow businesses to monitor, but not record, communications without consent:-

- to determine whether they are relevant to the business; and

- to monitor communications to a confidential anonymous counselling or support helpline.

One of the key requirements for relying on the Monitoring and Record-Keeping Regulations 2018 to monitor and record communications is that the employer makes all reasonable efforts to inform every person who may use the telecommunications system that interceptions may take place. This means, in practice, having a section on the company website referring to its IT usage policy, which addresses monitoring and storing of communications. The policy should explain fully what the purposes of any monitoring are, what is monitored and how the monitoring is carried out.

This information is important, as it defines the limits of the expectations of privacy that an employee may have. In the High Court case of Simpkin v Berkeley Group Holdings Plc [2017] EWHC 1472 (QB), an employee failed in arguing that his employer could not rely on documents that he said were confidential and that he had sent from his work account to his personal email account in order to send to his divorce lawyer, when:

- he had signed the IT policy that warned him that emails sent and received on its IT system were company property

- the employer's IT department and Mr Simpkin's personal assistant had access to all emails sent and received

- he had created the document in the course of his employment using his employer's IT system

There is no specific legislation in place within the UK governing an employee's right to privacy at work. However, **Article 8 of the European Convention on Human Rights** (ECHR) does state that "everyone has a right to respect for his private and family life, his home and his correspondence". This is not an absolute right though, and it applies only to public authorities. Even then, it has to be balanced against the demands of the general interest of the community and the requirements of the protection of the individual's fundamental rights.

Article 8 of the ECHR is incorporated into UK law by the **Human Rights Act 1998** and, although only public authorities (anybody carrying out functions of a public nature) are expressly subject to it, the courts must interpret all legislation consistently with ECHR rights. This would be relevant in an unfair dismissal claim arising from the monitoring of an employee's email communications, for example, where the employment tribunal would have to consider whether the dismissal was an interference with the employee's Article 8 rights when deciding whether the employer acted reasonably.

In such a case, the dismissal would be deemed to be unfair if interference with the employee's right to privacy was not justified.

The use of artificial intelligence

Artificial intelligence (AI) can be a very useful tool for carrying out assessments for recruitment and promotions. It may be used by an employer to sort through a large number of job applications, or to assess answers to psychometric tests, for example. AI has the ostensible advantage of promoting equality, transparency and accountability.

However, if AI is used injudiciously, the employer risks causing significant injustice. A tragic example of this is the use by the Dutch government in 2013 of an algorithm to assess recipients of child benefits to predict who was most likely to commit fraud. Risk factors such as low incomes and dual nationality were used. Unfortunately, the government did not investigate whether the algorithms were accurate, and wrongly accused and penalised around 26,000 parents, requiring them to pay back allowances that had been received over many years in their entirety. This drove many families into severe hardship, and more than 1,000 children were placed into foster care unnecessarily.

That is an extreme example, and a more mundane possible consequence in the workplace of the misuse of AI is likely to be a failure to recruit or promote someone. This can give rise to claims of unlawful indirect discrimination.

Indirect discrimination occurs where a person (in this case, Jack) applies to another person (in this case, Jill) a **provision, criterion or practice** (a PCP) that is discriminatory in relation to a relevant protected characteristic Jill has (such as her age, sex, disability or religion).

A PCP is discriminatory if:

- Jack also applies it to persons with whom Jill does not share the characteristic

- the PCP puts persons with whom Jill shares the characteristic at a particular disadvantage when compared to persons with whom she does not share it

- it causes or would cause Jill to suffer that disadvantage

- Jack cannot show the PCP to be a proportionate means of achieving a legitimate aim (called the 'justification defence')

This is best illustrated with a (somewhat silly) example. Say Jack owns a company and is considering promoting someone to production manager. There are four people in the running. However, he stipulates that he will only recruit someone with a "deep, commanding voice" (thereby applying the PCP of voice pitch). That PCP would disproportionately disadvantage most women, as most women cannot be said to speak with deep voices, an attribute usually associated with men. As Jill is a woman (thereby sharing the protected characteristic of sex) and speaks with a higher-pitched voice, she would suffer the same disadvantage as most of the other women.

Jack's reason is that he speaks with a deep voice and likes his senior managers to do the same, as it creates a "masterful, commanding impression for staff and clients". That's not a legitimate aim, so Jill has been indirectly discriminated against in relation to her sex. Even if the aim was legitimate, Jill's PCP would not be a proportionate means of achieving it.

The risk of indirect discrimination is prevalent in the use of AI tools, as they will mostly use algorithms that are bought off the shelf with 'rules' that are hidden but nonetheless amount to a PCP.

An algorithm is a set of rules that an AI process uses to carry out a task. At a very simple level, an algorithm may sort applications into order of date received, for example. However, in order for a more sophisticated tool to work, the algorithm needs to be fed a large corpus of data so it can 'learn'. For example, it could be used to sift through hundreds of applications received in response to a job advert, looking for those that most closely fit the criteria for the role. The obvious risk with this, though, is that the output of the algorithm will be entirely dependent on the rules of the algorithm and the inputted data.

So, if the data is out of date from the point of view of what is acceptable recruitment practice, the results will be skewed or biased. For example, if a company inputs data from the CVs of all of its successful hires between 2000 and 2020, it may well be the case that the algorithm will associate success with being male and white and/or having attended an Oxbridge college. Obviously, a large business may have the resources to correct such biases, but a smaller business may not. In addition, many of these packages are developed in the United States, where a different set of recruitment laws and conventions apply.

The obvious solution is to thoroughly understand how the AI tool works. If you do not, then an up-to-date British tool that expressly warrants that it complies with UK employment law and good practice is obviously to be preferred. Secondly, if possible, a cross-check should be carried out by a human, even if only done on a sample of the data, to ensure the algorithm is working in line with the policies of the business and current laws and good practices.

With psychometric tests, AI should never be relied upon solely, and it should be used simply as a tool.

·

Chapter 11
Summary

There is an age-old adage that a bad workman blames his tools. This applies equally to the modern world of IT. As essential and life-changing as IT is nowadays, if it is used improperly, it can cause a world of pain, including data protection breaches, compromised IT systems, damaged reputations, bullying and harassment claims, constructive dismissals, discrimination claims and even criminal prosecutions.

The answer is essentially three-pronged. Employers should:

- install robust and dynamic security measures, both technical and HR-driven to protect the organisation from ill-intentioned actions.

- ensure that clear, unambiguous rules and guidance are available to all workers, whatever their status, in order to both set the boundaries and give employers the right to take action if the rules are broken. Policies should be comprehensive, regularly disseminated and kept under frequent review to ensure they keep pace with both the rapidly changing world of technology and changing practices in the organisation.

- develop protocols for mitigating damage if and when a problem arises.

Also by
Daniel Barnett

Available on Amazon
or visit
go.danielbarnett.com/books

JOIN DANIEL EVERY SATURDAY EVENING AT
9PM WHEN HE PRESENTS THE ALL-NEW

LBC LEGAL HOUR

— OR CATCH UP VIA THE GLOBAL PLAYER,
AT bit.ly/lbclegalhour

SATURDAYS, 9PM

IMMEDIATE ACCESS
TO PRAGMATIC & PRACTICAL
HR & EMPLOYMENT LAW ADVICE
YOU CAN
IMMEDIATELY
PUT TO USE FROM
THE **SHARPEST** THOUGHT LEADERS
& HR PROFESSIONALS IN THE UK

FROM THE DESK OF DANIEL BARNETT

May 2022

Dear HR Professional,

You've got so many things going on at work.

The tricky HR issues you have to handle take up your time, your energy and your brain power. It can be exhausting to work under that level of pressure.

Maintaining your high standards of professionalism can be a real struggle, especially when your efforts and expertise often go unappreciated.

You have to make decisions on challenging HR situations you've sometimes never encountered before. Even if you're part of a team, it can feel like you're working in isolation.

With so much complexity and ambiguity, it's not always clear whether you're doing the right thing when there is so much to think about.

It can be draining. You've got to make tough decisions which may be unpopular. You need to ensure people are treated fairly while the business complies with its legal obligations. You've got pressure coming at you from all sides.

Doubt can creep in. What if you've got it wrong? You might even begin to question yourself.

You've got to cope with all that, whilst constantly having to convince any doubting stakeholders you're adding value to the business.

That's where the HR Inner Circle comes in. It's designed to ease that pressure by giving you swift access to resources and practical guidance you can implement right away.

Information I know that saves you time, energy and effort; resources packed full of practical, actionable advice that's difficult to find anywhere else; and a vibrant, active community of caring, like minded HR professionals willing to help you.

It's so easy to find what you want. And it doesn't matter what you're working on.

Whether it be workforce engagement, attracting and keeping talent, diversity and inclusion or employee health and well being, you'll find support for all of that.

You're covered even if you're working on one of those tricky, sensitive, people problems you never see coming until they land squarely on your plate.

Timely Support To Make Your Job Easier, Can Be Rapidly Found In The HR Inner Circle

As a member of the HR Inner Circle, all you have to do is ask. Or just do a quick search in the members' area (more about how easy that is in a moment).

Your first port of call is the vibrant Facebook group, bursting at the seams with incredible HR professionals like you. Just post your question and let it bubble and simmer in the collective genius of the group.

By the end of the day, you'll have at least 3-5 comments on your post, often more. You'll get relevant, insightful and practical guidance that comes from the hard earned experience of your fellow members.

Often you'll get a response within a couple of hours. Sometimes you'll get an answer within minutes - even if it's late in the evening!

This highly active community never fails to astound with just how willing they are to help fellow HR professionals like you by sharing their knowledge and experience.

> "Just Join. The Information and updates from the HR Inner Circle are excellent as well as the Facebook group where you can ask other members for advice which if you work alone is great as sometimes you just need to sense-check things."

Nicky Gleadow, HR Professional

> "If you're looking for a forum to discuss confidential issues and need prompt employment law advice then the HR Inner Circle is definitely for you. In addition it offers other tools to help and support. The Facebook group is full of information and solutions to scenarios invaluable for HR professionals".

Sheena Doyle, HR Professional

While you wait for your answer from the Facebook group, you can also search the members' vault in our secure online portal. It takes just 2 clicks and a quick keyword search using our Rapid Results Search Tool.

Instantly, you'll find exactly where your topic is covered in our extensive back catalogue of monthly magazines and audio seminars. One more click and you're straight there. In under 30 seconds you can find exactly what you're after. It's that quick and easy.

If you need a specific legal insight, pose your question live to an expert employment lawyer in our monthly Q&A session.

It'll either be me or one of my prominent contemporaries. Get your answer immediately without having to pay any legal costs.

A quick search of the previous Q&A sessions, and you'll find where it's been answered before. Our clever index system means you can find a question, and in one click get straight to the answer.

But perhaps you need to dive deep and explore the different options open to you?

Then join one of our monthly HR Huddles. There you can run your specific situation past other HR professionals. They'll offer their insights, share their experience and work WITH you to find a solution that works FOR you.

It's A Labour Of Love Putting All This Together For You.

I've spent years practising law and have become recognised as one of the UK's leading employment law barristers. I've even got my own radio show! But more importantly for you, I've also developed another skill.

It's bringing employment expertise AND practical experience together in a way that supports busy, overworked (and sometimes stressed) HR professionals like you.

Being a member now means your business and clients will see you as even more informed about the intricacies of employment law. They'll marvel at how well you keep up to date when you're so busy working hard for them.

You'll be seen making quicker decisions and implementing solutions that will accelerate the growth of the organisation. You'll make impressive time and cost savings for the business.

And those tricky, off-piste situations you've never come across before? Well, nothing will faze you, because you're backed up by an HR support system second to none.

But more importantly, you'll feel that pressure gently ease off.

That's Why I'm Inviting You To Reap The Many Rewards Of Membership

Here's what you get when you join the HR Inner Circle:

 Firstly, you'll get unlimited access to the hugely popular HR Inner Circle Facebook Private Group (Value: £1,188.00 a year)

- Tap into the vast wealth of knowledge, experience, insight and wisdom of the top 0.5% of your profession at any time, day or night.

- In less than 5 minutes you can post ANY HR question and get insightful answers and suggestions in a couple of hours or less, from some of the best in your profession.

- Fast track your impact by discovering effective shortcuts and workarounds from people who've been "there" and done "it".

- Expand and deepen your network of like minded individuals, secure in the knowledge they're as dedicated and as ambitious as you.

- Increase your prestige with your colleagues and stakeholders by being part of such an exclusive and prominent HR community.

- Gain confidence in your judgment and decisions by using the highly responsive community as a sounding board for your ideas.

"The HR Inner Circle is fantastic support for HR Professionals. The Facebook group is a great sense check when you work on your own and a great way to get a different perspective.."

Nancy Prest, HR Professional

"The HR Inner Circle is the best CPD investment you can make. Regardless of how you learn best, there is something for everyone and you're always up to date about employment law, case law and the subtle gray areas in between. If it's not already written down, just ask the group and someone will have the answer."

Lara Kenny, HR Professional

"The HR Inner Circle is an extremely helpful forum in which to bounce around ideas with very knowledgeable and experienced HR professionals and ask for advice and views on employment relations issues."

Yolaine Bech, HR Professional

2 Secondly, you'll receive 11 copies of the HR Inner Circular Magazine every year (Value: £350.00 annual subscription)

- Enjoy that satisfying "THUD" on your door mat every month when the postman delivers your very own copy of the HR Inner Circular magazine.

- Quickly discover exactly what the law says about key issues affecting HR professionals around the UK who are just like you.

- Get concise and practical guidance on how employment law applies to the challenging situations and circumstances you deal with every day.

- Avoid the mistakes of others by applying the lessons from the in depth analysis of real life case studies.

- Benefit from a legal deep dive by the UK's leading employment law barrister into a topical employment question posed by a fellow member (perhaps you!).

- Review a summary of recent important Facebook Group discussions worthy of sharing, that you may have missed.

- Learn from a range of related and relevant topics useful for your practice and your broader professional development.

"I thoroughly recommend the HR Inner Circle. It's worth every penny from the monthly magazine to the weekly podcast to the monthly audio seminars. And just having the support network to call on for a comfort blanket from time to time. I've been a member since it started"

Alison Melville, HR Professional

3 Thirdly, you get an exclusive invite to a live online Q&A Session every month, led by an expert employment lawyer
(Value: £199.00 a session or £2,388 a year)

- Gain 60 minutes of live and direct access to the sharpest legal minds from my secret little black book of contacts.

- Get answers to your knottiest employment law questions, and solutions to your trickiest HR problems, from some of the brightest employment lawyers in the UK.

- Avoid having to pay the £300-£400 it would cost you to ask a lawyer your question outside of the HR Inner Circle.

- Benefit from valuable insights from the answers given to other members.

- If you can't attend live, watch the recording when it's convenient for you.

- Quickly access the recorded answer to any question asked in the session by simply clicking the question index for that session.

- Save time by downloading the session transcription to scan-read at a time suitable for you.

> *"The HR Inner Circle gives you access to Daniel's practical and straightforward advice on employment issues. The businesses I work with don't want jargon, they just want pragmatic advice and I can access that through HR Inner Circle"*

Mandy Carr, HR Professional

> *"It's a breath of fresh air to have an HR resource which gives practical advice and tips. We can find out the law but it's the application of the law and HR practice led by a barrister along with the opinions of other HR professionals in the Q&A sessions which are invaluable "*

Caroline Robertson, HR Professional

 Fourthly, Join a live Monthly Huddle with other HR Professionals to solve your most challenging HR problems (Value: £1,188.00 a year)

- Attend your very own mini-mastermind group of highly qualified, highly regarded and experienced fellow HR professionals to "group think" through an issue you're facing right now.

- Develop bespoke solutions to the unique problems and challenges you have to deal with in a safe, supportive and confidential environment.

- Feel safe knowing these online zoom calls are NOT recorded to respect the sensitivity of issues addressed and the privacy of those involved. [NOTE - a professional transcriber attends and takes written notes. An anonymised summary is then made available to the membership]

- Recent Huddle topics included changing employee benefits, mandatory vaccination, career breaks, sickness during disciplinaries, effective worker forums and hybrid working arrangements.

"The HR Inner Circle is a great network opportunity to get practical and refreshing approaches for day to day HR and employment law matters. It's great to see that we all experience tricky cases from time to time"

Annabel Carey, HR Professional

"HR can be a lonely role and as the person advising everyone around you, it can often be difficult to find advice and peer support for you as an individual. We all know there are rarely right and wrong answers in HR. It's an art not a science and the HR Inner Circle gives you a group of like minded individuals to share solutions, provide expertise and insight, and a place to go when you just don't have the answers. "

Jo Mosley, HR Professional

> *"Lots of HR professionals work in standalone in-house roles or their own consultancy. We all need to stay relevant and get an occasional sanity check on a project and bounce around ideas and problems off others. So joining the HR Inner Circle to find a group of like minded professionals is essential in my view."*

Vanessa Scrimshaw, HR Professional

5 And finally, Your Personal Concierge will help you get the best out of your membership (Value: Priceless!)

- You get personal access to a personal concierge who'll point you in the direction of exactly where to find what you need. She's supported hundreds of members over the years she's been at my side.

- She also works closely with the 11 back office staff that support the operation. In the extremely unlikely event she doesn't know where something is, she knows who will.

> *"Use everything in the HR Inner Circle and you'll get the best possible support. The Magazine and the Audio Seminars keep me up to date and I can give something back and learn a few things on the Facebook group."*

Michelle Kirk, HR Professional

"The Inner Circle is a forum where you can get HR advice in all different formats. The monthly magazines and the audio seminars, the Facebook group and the annual conference. It is excellent value for money."

Christine Cooper, HR Professional

"Just join. The resources available to the HR Inner Circle members are invaluable especially the Facebook group where you can get advice or a different point of view that you may not have previously considered outside of normal working hours which is really useful. Live Q&As too."

Diana Wilks, HR Professional

How Much Does joining the HR Inner Circle Cost?

Let me remind you of the annual value of membership you get when you join:

Access to the private Facebook Group	£ 1,188.00
HR Inner Circular Magazine subscription	£ 350.00
Live Q&A sessions	£ 2,388.00
Monthly HR Huddles	£ 1,188.00
Your Personal Membership Concierge	PRICELESS!

TOTAL   £ 5,114.00

But you're not going to pay anywhere near that. **All it's going to cost you is just £96 +VAT per month. That's the equivalent of the price of a daily Starbucks.**

Another way of looking at your investment is this:

It's like having your very own part time, legally trained, assistant HR Business Partner, just waiting to provide you with all the answers you need…. **all for just £96+VAT per month.**

And that price is fixed for as long as you remain a member.

Plus, With Membership Of The HR Inner Circle, You'll Also Get These 6 Bonuses
Worth £3,305.00 For FREE!

Bonus #1: Free Access To The Annual Conference every May (Value: £399)
The perfect opportunity to extend your personal network and gather key insights and takeaways to help you personally and professionally. Includes lunch too.

Bonus #2 - Monthly Audio Seminars (Value: £588.00)
A 60 minute legal deep dive by me into an important subject relevant to you and your practice every month (downloadable mp3).

Bonus #3 - Handling Awkward Conversations (Value: £997.00)
A video case study masterclass you can share with managers to train them to handle awkward staff disciplinary, performance and attitude problems.

Bonus #4 - 4 x HR Employment Online Courses (Value: £388.00)

Deconstructing TUPE, Changing Terms & Conditions, Unconscious Bias At Work and Handling Grievances.

Bonus #5 - Free listing on the Register of Investigators (Value: £250.00)

Advertise your professional investigations service in our member's portal

Bonus #6 - Significant Discounts On My Flagship Products (Value: £683.00)

Get member discounts on my Getting Redundancy Right and HR Policies products as well as other price reductions as new products are released.

I'm So Confident Joining The HR Inner Circle Is The Right Decision For You, Here's My 100% Satisfaction "Buy It Back"

Guarantee

Take action and join the HR Inner Circle now. If you're not 100% satisfied with your investment after 30 days, I'll refund and buy EVERYTHING back from you.

I'm comfortable doing this because I know once you join, you'll find the support, the information and the strategies so useful, you'll never want to leave.

Before you decide though, let me be very clear about membership of the HR Inner Circle.

It's only for ambitious and dedicated HR professionals who want to accelerate and increase their impact by plugging into an HR ecosystem with its finger firmly on the pulse of what's working right now in HR. If you're just plodding along and are content with just getting by, then this is probably not for you.

But if you're drawn to benefiting from standing shoulder to shoulder with some of the giants in the HR community, then re-joining the HR Inner Circle is the RIGHT decision for you. Join here now:

www.hrinnercircle.co.uk

Daniel Barnett

PS after you join www.hrinnercircle.co.uk, if you don't feel it's right for you, we'll refund anything you've paid if you ask within 30 days.

If you are looking for a forum to discuss confidential issues that need prompt employment law advice, then the HR Inner Circle is definitely for you. In addition it offers other tools to help and support. The Facebook group is full of information and solutions to scenarios — invaluable for HR professionals.

- **Sheena Doyle**, Managing Director, The Really Useful HR Company Ltd

It's a forum where you're not afraid to ask stupid questions, even though I'm not usually afraid of doing that. The sheer variety of experience and skillsets ensures there is always an informed discussion. JOIN NOW!!

- **Jon Dews**, HR & Business Partner, Majestic 12 Ltd

If you are looking for a steady stream of thorough, pragmatic, and easily-digestible employment law advice, the HR Inner Circle is a great place to be.

- **Susi O'Brien**, Senior Manager HR, The Action Group

The regular updates are invaluable to not only me, but also my team. We find that they are presented in an easy to digest format and aren't too 'legalistic'.

- **Donna Negus**, Sekoya Specialist Employment Services

WWW.HRINNERCIRCLE.CO.UK

There aren't many other employment law advice services where you get direct access to an employment law barrister at a realistic price. Join the HR Inner Circle now – you won't regret it.

- **Kirsten Cluer**, Owner of Cluer HR, HR Consultancy

I like being able to use the HR Inner Circle Facebook group to ask other members for a second opinion, or for ideas when I get stuck with solving a tricky situation. There's usually someone who has come across the situation before.

- **Helen Astill**, Managing Director, Cherington HR Ltd

When I transitioned from big employers to an SME, I didn't realise how much I would miss having peers to kick ideas around. If you haven't got an internal network, you've got to build an external one. I got so much out of the discussion at an Inner Circle meetup recently and I look forward to getting the Inner Circular.

- **Elizabeth Divver**, Group HR Director, The Big Issue Group

Sign now! The monthly Q & A sessions are invaluable, the magazine is packed full of helpful info, you get lots of goodies and the Facebook page is really informative and a useful sounding board.

- **Caroline Hitchen**, Consultant, Caroline Neal Employment Law

WWW.HRINNERCIRCLE.CO.UK

Being a member of HR Inner Circle is one of the best sources of HR information and advice, and receiving the monthly audio seminars and magazines is extremely helpful and interesting. I can't recommend becoming a member highly enough. There is a private Facebook group which is great for asking other members advice and sharing knowledge and experiences. I have also recently attended one of the meetups that is organised by Daniel Barnett, and it was good to meet other members (and of course Daniel) in a more social setting. It was also a good opportunity to ask any questions you wanted and being able to get advice or support as to how they would deal with whatever you ask.

- **Tracey Seymour**, HR Manager (Head of Dept), Kumon Europe & Africa Ltd

The help and advice from other HR professionals on Facebook is really valuable, and quick. All the team enjoy the audio seminars and magazines for updates on current issues.

- **Catherine Larke**, Director | myHRdept.co.uk

WWW.HRINNERCIRCLE.CO.UK

For me it's a no brainer. We have a lot of really good contributors in the HR Inner Circle and it's more than a discussion forum and invaluable source of information. When combined with the magazine, the audio seminars and events, it is a complete service especially with Daniel's legal expertise always on hand.

- **Elizabeth Ince**, Self employed HR Consultant

Just join! It is invaluable with the resources you have at hand by joining the HR Inner Circle. Especially the Facebook Group where you can get advice or a different point of view that you may not have previously considered, outside of normal working hours which is very useful. Live Q&A's too.

- **Diana Wilks**, HR Manager, Go South Coast Ltd

HR can be complex because each and every issue will have its own set of individual circumstances. Being in the HR Inner Circle enables you to bounce ideas around and make sure you are considering every angle and aspect, knowing your HR Inner Circle partners will have had a similar experience to share.

- **Pam Rogerson**, HR Director, ELAS Group